MAGNIFICENT TALES®

Treasury of Bible Stories

Rhythmical Rhymes of Biblical Times

Kelly Pulley

David C Cook®

transforming lives together

TREASURY OF BIBLE STORIES
Published by David C Cook
4050 Lee Vance View
Colorado Springs, CO 80918 U.S.A.

David C Cook Distribution Canada
55 Woodslee Avenue, Paris, Ontario, Canada N3L 3E5

David C Cook U.K., Kingsway Communications
Eastbourne, East Sussex BN23 6NT, England

LCCN 2014938524
ISBN 978-0-7814-0917-9

The Team: Don Pape, Ingrid Beck, Catherine DeVries, Amy Konyndyk, Karen Athen
Cover Design: Kelly Pulley

Manufactured in Dong Guan City, P.R. China, in May 2014 by South China Printing.
First Edition 2014

1 2 3 4 5 6 7 8 9 10

041714

For my wife, Vickie

Contents

The Payment for Our Sins

He Has Risen!

Tricked by a Snake
The Slippery Story of Adam and Eve
Based on Genesis 2—3

God made Adam a beautiful place to call home,
a garden with flowers and trees.
The garden of Eden had plants of all kinds
that swayed in the warm, gentle breeze.

There were tropical trees that had blankets of blooms;
some had fruit that was tasty and sweet.
There were apples and oranges, bananas and pears
and cherries for Adam to eat.

"You may eat from the trees in the garden," said God,
"except for the fruit of just one ...
the Tree of the Knowledge of Good and of Evil.
Eat *it* and your life will be done!"

God created a river to water the plants
so the garden was healthy and green.
And the bugs and the birds and the beasts lived there too—
the most beauteous place ever seen!

But Adam had work in the garden to do.
His job was to care for it all.
And to name all the bugs and the birds and the beasts,
every animal there, big and small.

For the odd-looking beasts with their noses stretched long,
the name *aardvarks* had just the right ring.
For the big, burly beasts with the horns on their heads,
the name *bison* seemed just the right thing.

He named humpity camels and web-footed ducks
and elephants, foxes, and goats—
and horses and inchworms and jackrabbits, too,
koalas and lambs with wool coats.

He named monkeys and newts.
He named owls that hoot hoots,
and penguins and quails and raccoons.
He named spiders and tigers all covered in stripes,
as umbrella birds sang happy tunes.

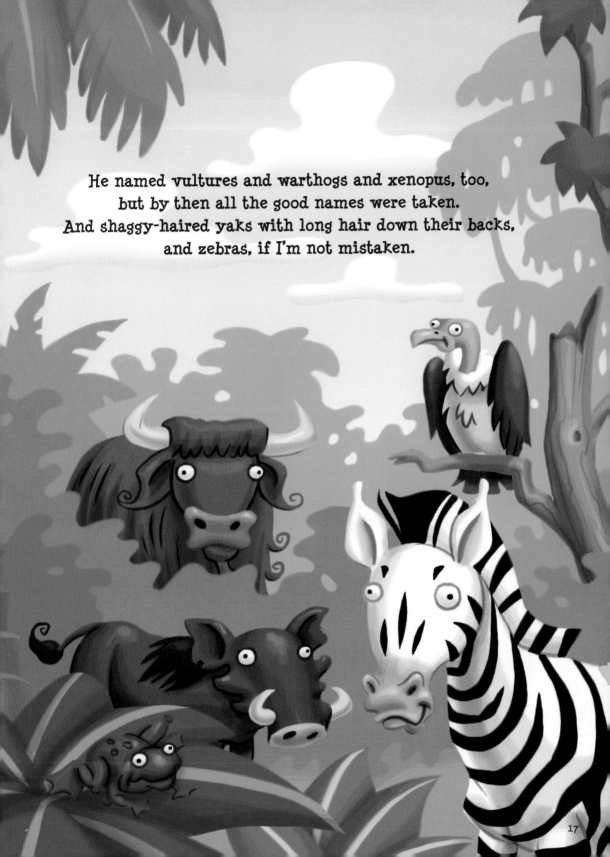

He named vultures and warthogs and xenopus, too,
but by then all the good names were taken.
And shaggy-haired yaks with long hair down their backs,
and zebras, if I'm not mistaken.

But with all of the bugs and the birds and the beasts,
still Adam was feeling alone.
God explained, "It's not good that he's here by himself.
I'll make Adam a friend of his own."

God put Adam to sleep. Then He took out a rib.
From the rib, God made Adam a wife.
The woman, named Eve, was a helper and more—
Adam now had a partner for life.

In the garden was everything either could want,
and life there was easy and fun.
They made friends with the bugs and the birds and the beasts—
every animal there, except one.

In the garden the snake was the trickiest thing.
He was ever so clever at cheating.
He hissed to the woman, "Did God really say
that none of this fruit is for eating?"

She answered, "It's fine if we eat from the trees.
But we *can't* eat the fruit of just one.
It's the Tree of the Knowledge of Good and of Evil.
Eat *it* and our lives will be done!"

"Your life won't be done," said the sly, sneaky snake.
"God knows it would make you like *Him*."
It looks tasty, she thought, *and the fruit makes you wise.*
So she picked off a piece from a limb.

Eve tasted the fruit. Then she gave some to Adam.
He took it. He tasted a bite.
At once, they could see that their bodies were bare.
And they wanted to hide from God's sight.

So they covered themselves with some leaves from the trees.
But as coolness was filling the air ...
they heard God, so they hid. God said, "Why did you hide?"
Adam answered, "My body was bare."

"Who told you you're bare? Did you eat from the tree?"
God added, "I told you, you couldn't!"
"The woman you made," Adam said, "it was she!
She gave me some fruit ... though she shouldn't!"

So God questioned Eve. But *she* blamed the snake.
The snake trembled, expecting the worst.
"For behaving so badly," said God to the snake,
"more than all of the beasts, you'll be cursed."

"You will crawl on your belly the rest of your life
and you'll choke on the dust as you do.
You will fear and despise all the people you see.
They will all feel the same about you."

Then God said to Adam and Adam's wife, Eve,
"Because you ate fruit from the tree ...
you must go from the garden of Eden for good.
Life is harder outside, you will see."

Their lives in the garden were easy and fun
till the two of them made a mistake.
They *should* have been doing what God said to do,
but instead they were tricked by a snake!

Every Beast Times Two
The Salty Tale of Noah's Ark
Based on Genesis 6—9

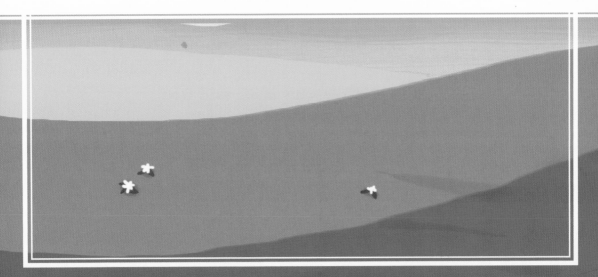

As people spread throughout the earth,
their numbers grew and grew.
And as the people numbered more,
their badness grew more too.

Their hearts grew hard and very cold.
All kindness was forgotten.
God's heart was filled with pain. He thought,
The earth has gotten rotten.

It really reeks!
It needs a bath!
So this is what I'll do—
I'll send a flood to wash it clean
and make the earth like new!

Now, Noah was a righteous man,
and Noah's heart was good.
He tried to live his life for God
and do the things he should.

"The earth is very bad," said God.
"The people there are mean.
I'll send a cleansing rain to flood
the earth and wash it clean."

"Go tell your sons, your wife, and theirs.
There's lots of work for you!
You need to build a great big ark,
for every beast times two!"

Now, Noah started right away.
He did as he was told.
The job was very, very big,
and he was very, very, very, very, very old.

He worked and worked and worked until,
at last, the ark was done.
Then, gathered every animal,
plus food for every one.

Some beasts were big and some were small.
Some scaly, some were furry.
Some slowly slithered on the ground.
Some flapped a feathered flurry.

They climbed aboard,
God closed the door.
Now they were safe within.
Then rain clouds started gathering.
The flood would soon begin.

At first a sprinkle,
then a splatter,
then splishing, splashing water!
The ark was tipping, tossing
like a tilting teeter-totter!

For forty days and forty nights
it rained on Noah's ark.
The raining stopped at last, and
sunshine chased away the dark.

For days and days they'd huddled close,
all cozy, safe, and well.
Now, men and beasts were getting bored,
and things began to smell.

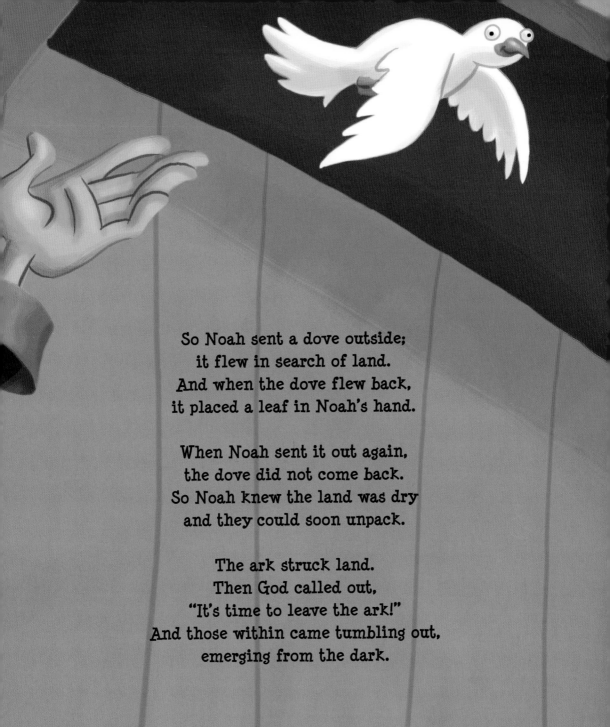

So Noah sent a dove outside;
it flew in search of land.
And when the dove flew back,
it placed a leaf in Noah's hand.

When Noah sent it out again,
the dove did not come back.
So Noah knew the land was dry
and they could soon unpack.

The ark struck land.
Then God called out,
"It's time to leave the ark!"
And those within came tumbling out,
emerging from the dark.

They stood outside.
They breathed the air—
air freshened by the storm.
The sunbeams streamed through clearing clouds.
The sun was bright and warm.

God placed a rainbow in the sky,
a sign for beasts and men
that He would never use a flood
to wash the earth again!

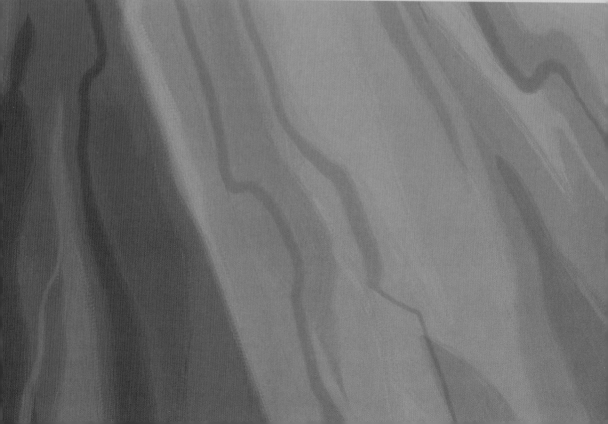

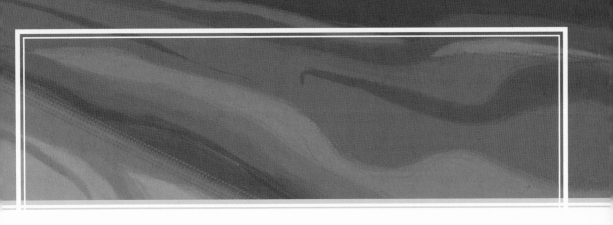

Dreams That Were Dreamed
The Colorful Story of Joseph and His Brothers

Based on Genesis 37—47

Jacob had sons who watched over his flocks,
as the sheep slowly grazed in the hills and the rocks.
He loved his son Joseph much more than the others.
So Joseph was hated by all of his brothers.

His brothers had *no* words of kindness to say.
Instead they sent insults and teasing his way.
Then when Jacob gave Joseph a robe like no other,
the others grew jealous of Joseph their brother.

And *then* Joseph spoke of a dream that he'd dreamed.
His brothers and he bundled grain, so it seemed.
His brothers' grain bundles all bowed while his stood.
His brothers all thought that his dream wasn't good.

Again, Joseph spoke of a dream that he'd dreamed.
The sun and the moon and some stars, so it seemed,
were bowing to Joseph while *he* stood up tall.
This angered his brothers. It made them feel small.

His father said, "What does this dream really mean?
Will *you* be our master? Is that what you've seen?"
His brothers were jealous. Their hatred grew hot.
Though Jacob loved Joseph, his brothers did not!

When the brothers were out with the sheep far away,
Jacob wanted to know if his sons were okay.
He sent Joseph to check. But his brothers were scheming.
They'd heard quite enough of the dreams he'd been dreaming.

They took Joseph's robe that he got from his dad.
They ripped it.
They tore it.
They made it look bad.

They took him and tumbled him into a well.
They planned to abandon him there where he fell.
But when traders passed near, with a shout and a wave,
they agreed to sell Joseph to them as a slave.

And that's what they did. Then they went to their dad.
They gave him the robe and they acted real sad.
Jacob cried, "A wild beast has made Joseph a snack!"
Then he wept for his son. Jacob wanted him back.

Meanwhile, Joseph was taken and put up for sale.
He was taken to Egypt and thrown into jail.
But Joseph had never done anything wrong.
Though his future looked bleak,
still his faith remained strong.

Then two jail mates were puzzled by dreams that they'd dreamed.
The dreams were a look at their futures, it seemed.
But the meanings weren't clear.
Were they bad? Were they good?
They asked Joseph to tell what they meant if he could.

He said one of the men would again be set free.
But the other would not.
No, he *never* would be.

Now, both of the men had once worked for the king.
When the one was set free, Joseph asked him one thing:
"Please, remember to talk to the king about me.
I've done nothing wrong, so he might set me free."

Joseph waited two years, but the man had forgotten.
Most people would say Joseph's luck had been rotten.
Though his future right then didn't seem very bright,
Joseph trusted that God would make everything right.

When the king became puzzled by dreams that he'd dreamed,
not one of his men could explain them, it seemed.
Then the man who'd forgotten remembered again
Joseph in jail from two years before then.

The king then told Joseph the dreams that he'd dreamed.
The first was a dream about cows, so it seemed.
Seven cows by the Nile that were healthy and brawny
were eaten by seven ... all tawny and scrawny.

The king then told Joseph his second strange dream.
The dream was a dream about grain, it would seem.
Seven heads on one stalk that were healthy and thick
were eaten by seven ... all skinny and sick.

Joseph said to the king, "Both the dreams are as one.
Seven years we'll have crops.
Seven years we'll have none."

The king then made Joseph his own right-hand man.
He put Joseph in charge of a fourteen-year plan
for storing the food and then handing it out,
so no one in Egypt would starve from the drought.

When later, the drought was quite bad all around,
where Jacob was living, no food could be found.
So his sons went to Egypt to buy what they needed.
They bowed to the ruler and humbly they pleaded.

Joseph thought of the dream he had dreamed long ago ...
his grain had stood high, as his brothers' bowed low.
Now just like the grain, Joseph's brothers kowtowed,
though none of them knew it was he as they bowed.

They bought food and went home, but they soon needed more.
So the brothers went back to get food as before.

When they stood before Joseph, he said, "I am your brother!"
His brothers were frightened. They looked at each other.
They thought he was angry with them for the past.
But Joseph was happy to see them at last.

He cried, "I am Joseph! There's no need to fear!"
Joseph wept, and he asked that his brothers come near.
"Don't be worried by things in the past, for time's shown
they were part of a plan only God could have known.

"God made good out of things that were bad, so it seemed,
by giving His guidance through dreams that were dreamed."

Jochebed's Secret Joy

The Stirring Story of Baby Moses in the Nile

Based on Exodus 2:1-10

When Joseph and all of his brothers grew old,
each one, in their time, passed away.
Their children grew older, and they all had kids,
so their numbers grew greater each day.

These people were known as the Israelites,
and their numbers kept growing and growing.
The new king of Egypt was worried and scared.
He wished that their growing was slowing.

He was frightened that all of the Israelites
might decide to get rid of their king.
So the king made them all into slaves on that day,
as a way to prevent such a thing.

Now they worked,
and they worked,
and they worked making bricks.
They were dirty and weary and sore.
But with God on the side of the Israelites,
their numbers grew more than before.

The king was so frightened he plotted a plan
that was evil and wicked and vile.
Any boys that were born to the Israelites
would be floated away down the Nile.

63

Now, Jochebed's secret was hidden away.
So the king wouldn't know what she had.
Her heart filled with joy for her new baby boy.
But still she was frightened and sad.

After hiding her baby away for three months,
God finally showed her a way
to save him from floating away down the Nile,
so she'd know that her boy was okay.

She wove a papyrus reed basket that day
and settled her baby inside.
She carefully set him adrift on the Nile,
where the water ran murky and wide.

Her daughter, named Miriam, watched from the shore
as the basket sailed by like a boat.
The princess was bathing downstream in the Nile
when she noticed the basket afloat.

She thought, *Why would a basket be floating out there?*
So she sent out a girl to retrieve it.
She opened the lid. She saw what it hid.
But the princess just couldn't believe it!

The baby inside looked so sad as he cried;
the princess felt bad for the baby.
She said, "He's a child of the Israelites."
Should I keep him? she thought.
I think, maybe.

Then Miriam went to the princess and said,
"Shall I find you a nurse for the child?"
Having planned all along to return with his mother,
she winked at the baby and smiled.

Although Jochebed's joy was her new baby boy,
to save him she gave him away.
Now her joy is no secret.
It shines every day.
Joy from God is a joy that will stay!

"Let My People Go!"
The Gripping Story of the Escape from Egypt

Based on Exodus 2:11—12:33

When Moses grew to be a man,
he looked around to see
his people being treated worse
than people ought to be.

In Egypt, all of them were slaves.
They worked both night and day
with barely any time to sleep
and never time to play.

When Moses tried to give them help,
the king got very mad
and Moses had to run away
and leave the life he had.

So Moses chose to shepherd sheep.
He started life anew
away from Egypt's wicked king
and safe from what he'd do.

And all the while, the people back
in Egypt prayed their prayers.
They prayed that God would set them free—
and claim some land as theirs.

As Moses watched his sheep one day,
he saw a bush that burned.
Then God said,"Moses! Moses!
It's time that you returned.

"I've heard the prayers My people prayed
and seen their sadness, too.
I've chosen you to set them free.
Now this is what you do ..."

God told him, "Go and tell the king
to let My people go.
So they can settle in the land
where milk and honey flow."

But Moses asked, "Lord, who am I,
that I should set them free?"
God answered, "I will be with you.
Just put your faith in Me."

Then Moses whined, "I can't speak well.
I think Your choice is wrong."
God said, "Your brother, Aaron, can,
so he should go along."

Then Moses went to see the king.
His brother went there, too,
with God's instructions what to say
and also what to do.

They told the king, "Our God has said,
'Now, let My people go.'"
The king said, "I don't know your God.
Go tell Him I said, 'No!'"

So Moses dropped his walking staff.
It turned into a snake.
The king was not impressed. He said,
"That snake is just a fake."

Now Moses took his staff and turned
the Nile a bloody red.
The king cried, "No!
They cannot go!"
He smirked and shook his head.

So God sent frogs from streams and bogs.
The frogs were everywhere.
They hopped in homes, on floors, in beds
and people's underwear!

The king cried, "All the slaves can go!
Just take the frogs away!"
But when the frogs were gone again,
he made the people stay.

So next, the Lord sent gnats, then flies.
Their animals got ill.

But still the wicked king said, "No!
The slaves must stay here still."

So Moses told the king again,
"Now let my people go!"
The king and everyone got boils.
But still the king said, "No!"

The Lord sent hail to hit their heads
and crush their crops below.
When Moses said to let them leave,
the king still answered, "No!"

The Lord sent lots of locusts,
lots of locusts everywhere.
The king said, "All the slaves can leave."
Again he kept them there.

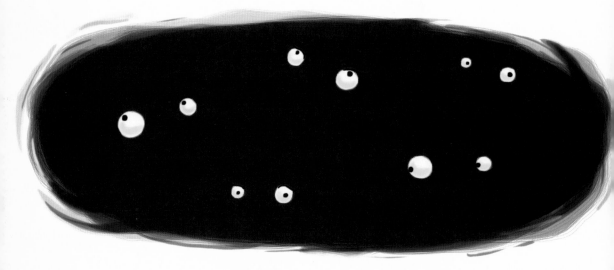

Three days the sky was dark as night,
Egyptians hid in fear.
But still the king stood fast and said,
"The slaves will all stay here!"

Then Moses told the wicked king,
"You'd better let them leave!
Or every firstborn here will die,
and everyone will grieve!"

But still he didn't let them go,
and so the firstborn died.
In Egypt every house was touched,
and everybody cried.

The king cried, "Moses, leave right now!
Get up! Get packed! Get out!
And take your people, flocks, and herds!
No time to hang about!"

Though Moses didn't think he could,
he followed God's own plan.
When God is on your side, you see,
then *can't* turns into *can!*

A Wall of Water
The Towering Tale of Moses Crossing the Sea
Based on Exodus 12:31—14:32

At last!
At last!
The slaves were free!
Now they at last could go.
So they could settle in the land
where milk and honey flow.

They packed their clothes.
They packed their kids.
They packed their cows and sheep.
They packed their goats.
They packed their food
stacked high in heaps to keep.

Then off they went to find their land,
with God to show the way.
A post of fire to lead by night,
a cloud to lead by day.

The people camped beside the sea.
They turned around to find
Egyptian soldiers and the king!
Again, he'd changed his mind.

God moved the cloud in front of them
to block the soldiers' sight.
God's people had to get away,
or they would have to fight.

Then Moses took his walking staff,
and, stretching out his hand,
he split the water in the sea,
which made a path of land.

A wall of water on their left
and water on their right.
The water towered high above.
It must have been a sight.

The people quickly got across,
the soldiers gaining fast.
But then the sea poured back on them.
The threat was gone at last.

The people all gave praise to God.
His goodness they could see.
In Egypt they had all been slaves,
but God had set them free!

A Silly-Sounding Plan
The Dizzying Tale of Joshua at Jericho

Based on Joshua 1—6

God's people had wandered for forty long years.
It was time that they had their own place.
God had promised a land that flowed milk and sweet honey,
where all would have plenty of space.

He made Joshua leader and put him in charge.
God promised to lend him a hand.
He said, "Over the Jordan, wherever you step,
is the place where you'll find your new land."

But the city of Jericho stood in their way.
It had walls that were sturdy and tall.
Before they could claim all the land as their own,
the walls and the city must fall!

Two spies sent by Joshua sneaked through the gate,
but the king somehow heard they were there.
A woman inside helped the two of them hide,
till the spies sneaked outside with great care.

They promised that all in her house would be safe,
then she told the two spies what she knew.
"The people of Jericho tremble with fear.
They know God and His strength are with you."

It was time for God's people to enter their land,
but the Jordan lay right in their way.
The river was deep and the water was fast.
But God's hand would make crossing okay.

When the priests with God's ark took a step in the river,
the water backed up and stopped flowing!
They stood in the middle to hold it all back
so that everyone else could keep going.

Now, when Joshua neared the tall walls of the city,
he noticed a man up ahead.
Then Joshua asked, "Are you friend? Are you foe?"
He said, "Neither ... I'm God's man instead."

Then the Lord said to Joshua, "Here is the city.
It's yours, if you do as I say.
Go gather the army and gather the priests.
Then march in exactly this way."

"Put some soldiers with swords marching out in the front
and in back, as a guard from attack.
Seven priests blowing trumpets in front of the ark.
Then circle the city and back.

"Do this once every day without speaking a word,
and repeat for six days in a row.
On day seven, you'll circle it seven full times.
Then you'll shout as the trumpets all blow."

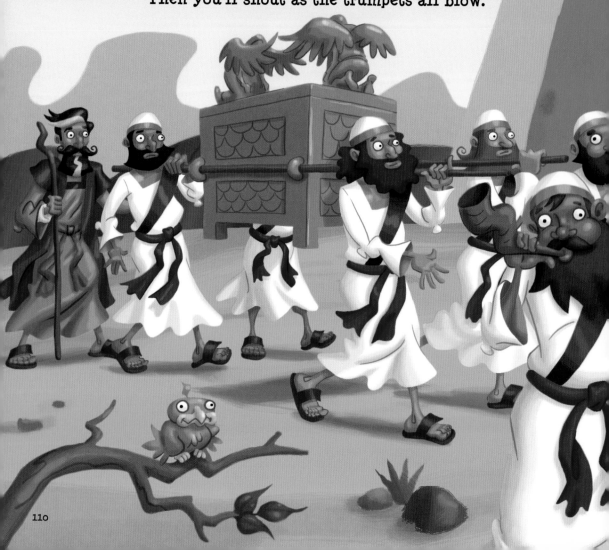

Though the plan sounded silly, the people obeyed,
because God always did as He said.
So all of the priests got in place in the line
with armed guards in the rear and ahead.

Then they marched around Jericho once every day,
and repeated—six days in a row.
On day number seven, they made seven trips
when they finally heard trumpets blow ...

Then Joshua ordered them, "Shout for the Lord!
He's given the city to you!"
Then Joshua shouted as loud as he could!
And the rest of the people did too!

They hollered and hooted and bellowed and yelled!
Soon Jericho's walls started shaking!
The priests blew their trumpets! The soldiers kept yelling!
The walls started cracking, then breaking!

The walls tumbled and fell! All the soldiers charged in!
The city was theirs as the prize!
God's plan may sound silly, but walls are no worry,
no matter their strength or their size!

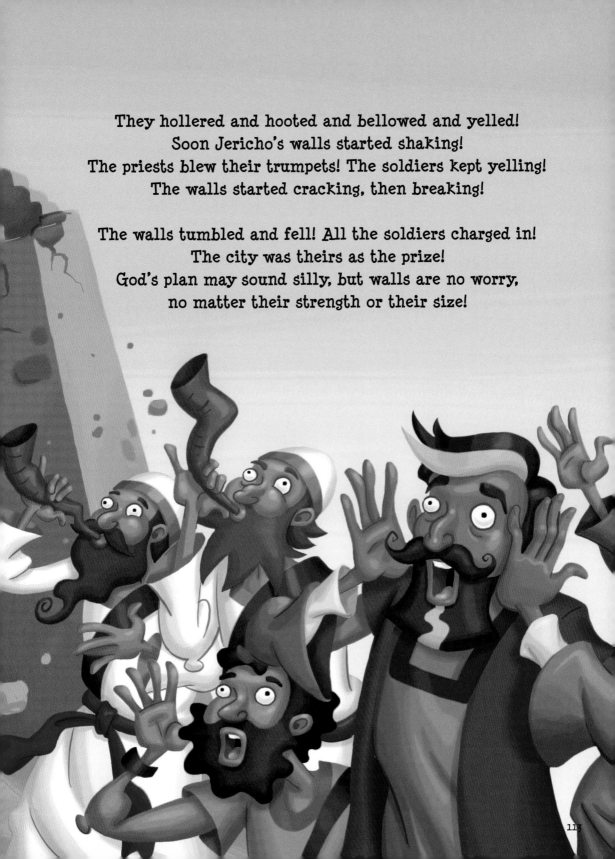

A Shout for the Lord
The Convincing Story of Gideon's Doubt

Based on Judges 6—7

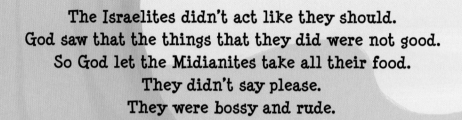

The Israelites didn't act like they should.
God saw that the things that they did were not good.
So God let the Midianites take all their food.
They didn't say please.
They were bossy and rude.

They took all the cows and the sheep and the wheat.
They took every bit and left little to eat.

After seven long years of them losing their food,
the Israelites were in such a bad mood.
They pleaded to God, as they should have done first.
"God, help us! Those Midianites are the worst!"

As Gideon secretly worked threshing wheat
by beating the wheat on the ground by his feet,
an angel said, "Warrior, God's on your side."
When Gideon heard this, he quickly replied,

"If God's on our side, tell me where has He been?
The bad guys grow fatter while we're getting thin."
So God said to Gideon, "Do as I say,
for *you* are the one who will drive them away."

But Gideon didn't believe what he'd heard.
Instead of believing, he doubted God's word.
He said, "Lord, are You sure that Your choice isn't wrong?
I'm *not* very brave, God.
I'm *not* very strong."

God said, "Go as you are. And with Me on your side
the enemy army will run and they'll hide."

Soon the enemy army invaded his land
while Gideon gathered more troops to command.
Still Gideon didn't believe what he'd heard.
Instead of believing, he doubted God's word.

"Please, show me a sign, then I'll know that You're right—
that it's *me* who You want,
that it's *me* who should fight.

"Make this wool become wet with the dew overnight,
but keep the ground dry, then I'll know that You're right."

And God did. Just like that.
And to stop any doubt,
the dew filled a bowl when the wool was wrung out.

But Gideon *still* wasn't sure. So he said,
"Let the wool remain dry—make the ground wet instead."
In the morning, the wool was completely dew-free,
while the ground all around was as wet as could be.

Now, Gideon's army was growing in size.
But God thought the army had too many guys.
He said, "Winning with too many men would be wrong.
They would think it was *them* and not *Me* who was strong."

God said, "Tell the men who are trembling with fear
to turn and go back.
There are too many here."

And he did. Now their number was less than before,
but God said again, "Let's get rid of some more."

He said, "Any who drink with their hands, let them stay.
If they drink like a dog, you should send them away."
So Gideon watched, and he counted each one.
Three hundred remained when his counting was done.

"With Me on your side and with you in the lead,
three hundred," God said, "is the number we'll need."
But Gideon *still* didn't trust what he'd heard.
Instead of believing, he doubted God's word.

God said, "Go to the enemy camp and you'll hear
that *you* are the one whom your enemies fear."
So Gideon sneaked to their camp in the night.
When he did, he discovered that God had been right.
The enemy soldiers were frightened to fight.

So Gideon gathered his three hundred men.
He told them the battle was soon to begin.
A horn and a torch
and a jar for each man.
Then he gave them instructions before they began.

"Watch me," he commanded, "and follow my lead.
We'll circle their camp using slyness and speed.
When all are in place and their camp is quite near,
we'll break all our jars and we'll shout so they'll hear,
'A sword for the Lord and for Gideon, too!'
Then we'll blow all our horns ... hold our torches up too!"

And they did. And the enemy army all cried!
And they ran for the hills!
And they all tried to hide!
And they ran, and they ran!
And they never returned!
Now Gideon thought of the lesson he'd learned.

When you're *not* very brave and you're *not* very strong,
God's plan may seem hard and a little bit wrong.
But if God's on your side, there's no reason to doubt.
Just blow on your horn, and praise God with a shout!

The Biggest and Toughest
The Story of David's Big Faith
Based on 1 Samuel 17

welcome
to the
WAR

The Philistine army stood facing King Saul.
They acted as though they weren't frightened at all.
But King Saul's mighty army was shaking with fear,
falling over each other to get to the rear.

There, standing in front of the Philistine camp,
was a giant, the Philistines' fierce fighting champ!
His name was Goliath, and, man, was he scary!
His muscles were huge! His body was hairy!
He stood nine feet tall, 'bout as tall as a tree!
The biggest man anyone ever did see!
The men in Saul's army, and even King Saul,
thought he was the biggest and toughest of all!

The giant cried, "Send me a soldier to fight!
I'll smash him all day and I'll stomp him all night!
When all of the smashing and stomping is through,
your land will be ours ... we'll make slaves out of you!"

For forty long days he repeated the call.
But no one would fight with him, no one at all.

David, a shepherd boy, shepherded sheep,
keeping beasties away so his sheep he could keep.
Though three of his brothers had gone with King Saul,
young David stayed home because he was too small.

His father gave David another big chore:
"Take food to your brothers out fighting the war."
Whatever his father would say, he'd obey,
so he packed up a donkey and went on his way.

When David arrived at the camp, he heard shouting—
mean insults and teases Goliath was spouting.

"Just when will you chickens send someone to fight?
I'll smash him all day and I'll stomp him all night!
When all of the smashing and stomping is through,
your land will be ours ... we'll make slaves out of you!"

welcome
to the
WAR

Again the king's soldiers went running in fear,
falling over each other to get to the rear.

David called to the soldiers, "Hey, who is that dude?
His insults are mean! His teasing is rude!"
"Goliath!" they shouted, while running away.
"He's big and he's tough, you'd be silly to stay!"

But David decided to talk to King Saul,
to tell him that *he* was not frightened at all.
The king said, "Goliath is big and he's tough—
you're a boy with a sling, that's not nearly enough!"
Young David said, "I fought a lion and bear!
Both were bigger than I, so the fights were not fair.
With God as my strength both the beasts took a beating!
With God as my strength I will *not* be retreating!"

The king said to David, "The Lord be with you.
Take my sword and my shield, put my helmet on too."
But the armor was big and the sword weighed a lot.
They fit on the king, but on David ... did not.
So off came the armor and all the king's stuff.
"With God as my strength just my sling is enough!"

He gathered some stones from the bed of a stream.
As he did, he could hear the big Philistine scream,
"I called for a soldier, you sent out a squirt!
Send him back to his mommy, he's gonna get hurt!
The boy is too puny to put up a fight!
I'll smash him all day and I'll stomp him all night!
When all of the smashing and stomping is through,
your land will be ours ... we'll make slaves out of you!"

Then David said, "You have your spear and your sword, but I will fight you *in the name of the Lord!*"

David loaded his sling and he spun it around.
The stone hit the giant ... then he hit the ground!

Now, the *Philistine* army went running in fear,
falling over each other to get to the rear.

Young David said, "*God* made the Philistine fall!
Because *God* is the biggest and toughest of all!"

God's Bigger Plan
The Beautiful Story of Queen Esther
Based on Esther 2—10

The king of the kingdom of Persia made known
that he needed a queen who could fill the queen's throne.
The king sent out searchers to search all around
and bring back the beautiful women they found.

Nearby, Mordecai lived with his cousin, young Esther.
With courage and kindness and beauty God blessed her.
Though Esther was Jewish, and Mordecai, too,
where they lived it was safer if few people knew.
When the searchers met Esther, they thought she was sweet,
the type of a girl that the king ought to meet.

With maidens to help her to look at her best,
she was powdered and pampered and painted and dressed.
She was primped and perfumed and her hair done in curls.
Then they placed her in line with the rest of the girls.

The girls met the king, one by one, girl by girl.
Every girl like the last; the king's mind was a whirl.
But Esther was sweeter than others he'd seen.
The king thought that Esther might make a good queen.
And that's just what happened.
She'd passed every test.
She'd won the queen's crown over all of the rest.

Now, Haman was known as the king's right-hand guy.
The people all bowed as he strutted on by.
They kneeled in respect,
which made Haman feel great!
But Mordecai wouldn't,
which filled him with hate!

And Haman was mean.
He disliked every Jew—
but Mordecai more than the others he knew.
He schemed up a plan to make Mordecai crawl.
And once and for all do away with them *all*!

So he went to the king with the plan that he had.
He said, "King, there are people out there who are bad.
The Jews are the worst!
No, they're not very nice!
Let's be rid of them all!
That's my humble advice."

The king trusted Haman.
So *he* got his way.
The king signed the law to make Jews go away.

Now, Mordecai heard about Haman's dark plot
to get rid of the Jews, and it scared him a lot!
He sent word to Queen Esther to tell her the plan
so that she could prevent it before it began.
He said, "Go to the king; it's the right thing to do—
or the Jews will be gone,
which means *you'll be gone too!*"

173

But to go uninvited to speak to the king
was unlawful to do and a dangerous thing!
He said, "God made you queen long before this began
to save all the Jews. It was God's bigger plan."

Queen Esther quite bravely approached the king's throne.
With God by her side Esther wasn't alone.
But the king wasn't mad—he was glad she was there.

So Esther spoke up, and she asked if he'd care
to come to a banquet that she would prepare.
She asked that the king would have Haman come too.
"At the banquet," she said, "I'll explain this to you."

So the king and Queen Esther and Haman all dined.
They sat at the table, relaxed and reclined.

The king questioned Esther and said, "Please explain."
She said, "Plans are in play that will cause my heart pain.
My people and I are in danger, I fear.
If the plans are not changed, we will all disappear."

"Who planned such a sinister plot?" the king cried.
Esther answered, "He's sitting right *there* by your side!"
She pointed to Haman.
His face went all white!
The king was so mad!
Haman trembled with fright!

"Take Haman away!" called the king to his men.
So that's what they did.
No one saw him again.

Mean Haman had failed at his sinister plot.
The Jews were still there.
But Haman was not.
So Mordecai stayed as the king's right-hand man,
thanks to Esther believing in God's bigger plan.

Daniel for Lunch
The Tasty Tale of Daniel in the Lions' Den
Based on Daniel 6

The work of a king can be hard and demanding,
so King Darius wanted some help with commanding.
He gathered some helpers to lend him a hand.
They cared for his stuff. They protected his land.

A worker named Daniel was clearly the best,
so the king made him boss over all of the rest.
But the rest were not happy with Daniel, their boss.
The king, they agreed, should give Daniel the toss!

They said, "Daniel must go,
then the choice will be clear
whom the king should make boss
from the helpers still here!"

They watched Daniel to see if he did something bad.
They would run and they'd tattle on him if he had.
They watched night. They watched day.
But they never did find
even one little thing
that would change the king's mind.

They whined, "Daniel is faithful,
he's good, and he's wise.
He *always* works hard,
and he *never* tells lies.
If there's one little thing we might use, then it's this:
He prays every day. Not a day does he miss."
"That's it!" said a helper.
"We've got him! He's through!
We'll make praying a crime!
Yes, that's *just* what we'll do!
We'll bamboozle the king into making it wrong,
then Daniel, our boss, won't be boss for too long!"

So they ran to the king, feeling ever so clever.
They greeted the king, saying, "King, live forever!
All we helpers agree that a law should be made
that says people who pray any prayers
that are prayed,
must pray them to *you* because *you* are the best!
They must *not* pray to men or
to gods or the rest!

"If they dare say a prayer to some other than you,
then they'll sleep with the lions!
Have lunch with them too!"

King Darius liked how the law made him feel.
So he wrote it all down and he gave it his seal.
Now the law had been signed. It could not be undone.
The helpers all grinned. Surely Daniel was done.
The law was proclaimed. One and all understood.
They must pray to the king. Hungry lions weren't good!

Now when Daniel got home, he did just as before.
He went straight to his window
and knelt on the floor.

He prayed only to God. Daniel broke the king's law,
as the helpers who spied while he prayed clearly saw.

Now they questioned the king,
feeling ever so clever,
"Can the law be undone?"
And the king answered, "Never!"
They said, "Daniel still prays to his God every day!
He cares nothing for you or the things that you say!
He must sleep with the lions! The law is quite clear!
You signed it yourself! See, your seal is right here!"

So the king gave the order to some of his men,
that Daniel be thrown in the lions' dark den.
He was brought to the pit. Then they pitched him inside.
King Darius poked in his head as he cried,
"May your God whom you serve without cease every day
rescue you from the lions and keep you okay!"

Now the king was quite worried because of his hunch
that the lions were hungry and Daniel was lunch!
Too worried to sleep and too worried to eat,
when the sun began rising, he jumped to his feet.

He ran lickety-split to the den from his room.
He was worried that Daniel had met with his doom.

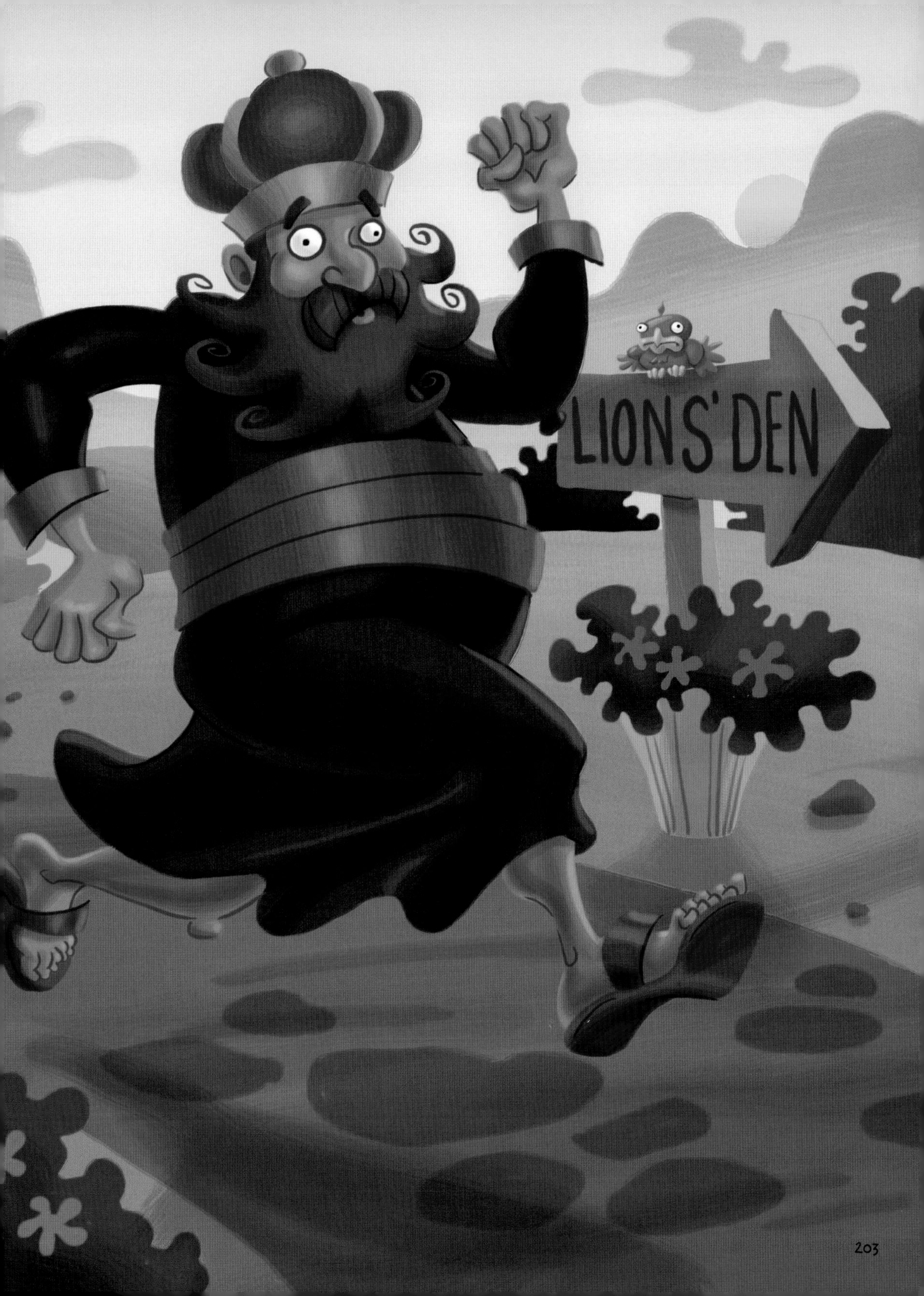
LIONS' DEN

"Did your God whom you serve keep you safe?"
the king cried.

"Yes, an angel from God saved me!" Daniel replied.
"He calmed all the lions so none would attack
and munch me for lunch or perhaps for a snack."

The king was delighted that Daniel was free!
To his kingdom the king then declared by decree,
"Whenever you pray any prayers that you pray,
no matter the place or the time of the day,
don't pray them to men! And don't pray them to me!
Just pray them to God, who let Daniel go free!
He calmed all the lions. He stopped their attack.
They didn't munch Daniel for lunch or a snack!"

Food for a Fish
The Whopping Story of Jonah and the Whale
Based on Jonah 1—3

God loves *all* of His people.
He loves them a lot.
The ones who do good
and the ones who do not.

The people of Nineveh
weren't doing good.
The things that they did
weren't the things that they should.

So God said to Jonah, "Please do what I say.
Go to Nineveh now! Leave at once! Don't delay!
Tell the people I love them and not to do bad,
or they will be punished, and I will be sad."

214

Jonah thought to himself,
A trip there won't be fun.
I will go somewhere else, like a beach in the sun.
The Nineveh people are grumpy and rude,
like they woke from a nap in a terrible mood.

Jonah liked his new thinking.
He liked it a lot.
"I'll hide out in Tarshish!
I know just the spot!

"I'll do what I want!
Do what I want to do!
All I need to escape
is a boat and a crew!"

So he sneaked on a boat,
which he thought was quite smart.
But God wasn't fooled,
for He *knew* Jonah's heart.

Then God made a storm,
and the rain began lashing!
The wind was whish-whooshing!
The waves were splish-splashing!

The boat started tilting and tossing about!
The sailors hung on so they wouldn't fall out!

All the sailors cried out,
"We must do something quick,
or this splishing and splashing
will make us seasick!"

So they ran to wake Jonah,
who slept down below.
"Tell us *what* we should do!
Tell us *now* so we'll know!"

"I've been running from God.
Now He's angry with me.
Throw me out of the boat.
Throw me into the sea."

So they did what he said,
and the rain stopped its lashing.
The wind stopped whish-whooshing.
The waves stopped splish-splashing.

All the sailors were happy,
but Jonah was not.
He was under the sea.
He was in a bad spot!

But God rescued Jonah
and granted his wish!
God spared him from drowning ...
inside a big fish!

Three days and three nights
he spent inside its belly.
It was damp,
it was dark,
and oh boy,
was it smelly!

Jonah knew he'd been wrong
to try running away.
So he looked in his heart
for the words he should say.
Then he lowered his head
and got down on his knees.
And he prayed prayers to God,
pleading, "God, hear me, please.
You saved me from drowning
here inside this fish.
I'll do what You want,
do whatever You wish."

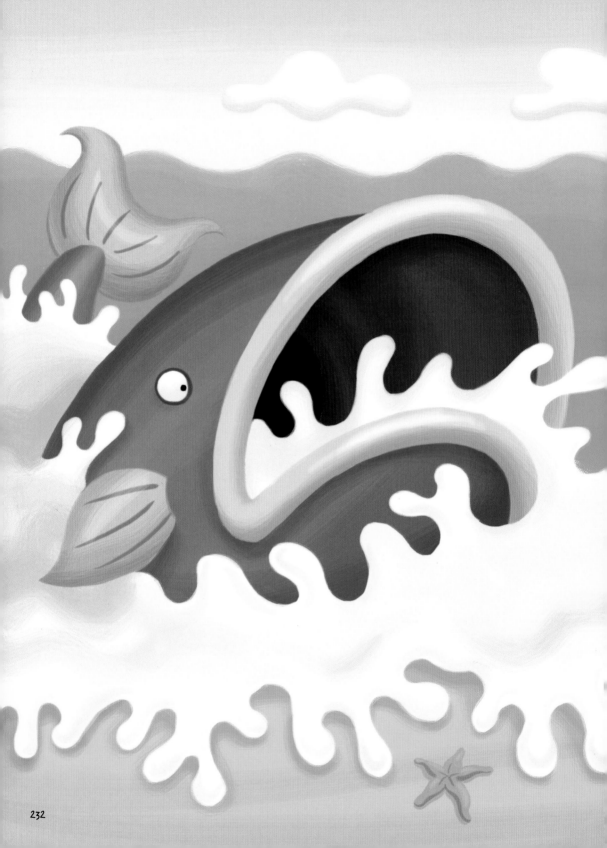

Then the fish spat him out.
Spat him onto dry land.
He was wet.
He was smelly
and covered with sand.

Jonah shook off the sand
with a brush and a flick.
Started walking to town,
started walking quite quick.

To the people he shouted
as loud as he could,
"Stop doing what's bad
and start doing what's good!
The Lord sent me here,
sent me here to this spot.
He told me to tell you,
He loves you a lot!"

The people all cheered,
for God's love they now knew.
Jonah thought to himself
that he'd learned something too ...

It's never too clever
to run from God's wish.
Or you just might end up
being food for a fish.

Good News of Great Joy
The Amazing Story of Jesus's Birth

Based on Luke 1:26—2:14

A young woman named Mary
got quite a surprise
when an angel appeared
right in front of her eyes!

She was terribly frightened
as you would be too
if what happened to her
had just happened to you!

The angel said,
"Mary, there's no need to fear.
You are special to God,
which is why I am here.
I bring you the message
that you are the one
who was chosen by God
to give birth to His Son."

Mary said, "I'm not married,
so how could this be?"
Then the angel told Mary,
"Trust God and you'll see."
So she trusted in God.
She said, "Lord, let it be."

Now, Mary and Joseph
were soon to be wed.
Joseph dreamed of an angel
while sleeping in bed.

He was terribly frightened
as you would be too
if what happened to him
had just happened to you!

The angel said,
"Joseph, there's no need to fear.
I've a message from God,
which is why I am here."

"The baby that Mary
now carries within
is Jesus,
God's Son,
who will pay for man's sin."

God's message was clear.
Joseph knew what to do.
So he married young Mary.
She married him, too.

Soon they both had to travel to Joseph's hometown,
so the king's people-counters
could write their names down.
To Bethlehem Joseph and Mary were sent,
so they packed up some things
on their donkey and went.

WELCOME
TO
BETHLEHEM

But the town was so crowded
there wasn't a room.
And the baby in Mary
was coming out soon!

Then the innkeeper said,
"There's a place you can rest.
As for beauty and comfort,
it's far from the best.

"It's a stable where horses
and cows and sheep stay.
But at least there's a roof
and some dry, comfy hay."

That night Jesus was born
in the animals' stable,
where Joseph and Mary
did what they were able
to make Him a cozy,
warm, comfortable bed,
in a manger with hay
they fluffed up for His head.

Then they wrapped Him up tight
in some soft swaddling clothes,
which made Him feel snug
from His head to His toes.

And the animals' lullabies
lulled Him to sleep,
with soft mooing of cows
and the bleating of sheep.

Nearby, shepherds were watching
their sheep in the night
when an angel appeared!
All around them shone bright!

They were terribly frightened
as you would be too
if what happened to them
had just happened to you!

The angel said,
"Shepherds, there's no need to fear.
I have brought you good news
of great joy you should hear!"

"Today in a manger
was born Christ the King!"
Then a great many more angels started to sing!
They appeared all around,
singing praises, and then
they sang, "Glory to God,
peace on earth to all men!"

The Good Dunking
The Refreshing Story of John the Baptist

Based on Matthew 3:1-17, Mark 1:4-11, Luke 3:2-22, John 1:6-34

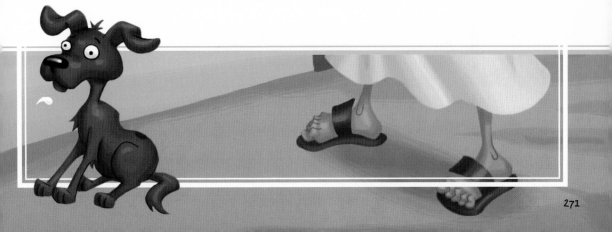

John came to the desert to baptize and teach,
with a message of hope and salvation to preach.

He wore camel-hair clothes and a belt 'round his waist,
a remarkable man with the simplest of taste.
And the food that he ate was a little bit funny,
some locusts for lunch and some sticky wild honey.

But people would come from the towns all around.
They'd travel for miles to where John could be found.
They'd sit for the message that John would deliver,
confess all their sins, and be dunked in the river.

Now some of the people thought John was the one
who they'd waited upon, perhaps God's very Son.
But John would explain he was just a plain guy.
"After me there will be someone greater than I,
whose sandals I'm not even fit to untie."

More people arrived at the river each day.
They confessed.
They got dunked.
Then they went on their way.

And then, on a day that was like any other,
John stood in the river and baptized another.
He looked for the next one when that one was through
and saw Jesus was standing in line, waiting too!
Then John told Him, "I should be baptized by You!"

275

But Jesus insisted that this was the way,
that this was the place,
and that this was the day.

John consented but couldn't help thinking it odd
that he would be dunking the one Son of God.
But when Jesus came up from the water and stood,
it was clear that the job John was doing was good.

For heaven was opened and down from above
came floating the Spirit of God like a dove,
and a voice saying, "This is My Son, whom I love."

A Better Path
The Miraculous Story of Jesus Walking on Water

Based on Matthew 14:22-33

His day of teaching was complete,
so Jesus took a break.
His helpers got into a boat;
they sailed across the lake.

Then Jesus climbed a hill to find
a quiet place to pray.
From high atop the hill He saw
His helpers sail away.

The sun went down,
then waves swelled up
when wind began to blow.
Ker-splish!
Ker-splash!
Ker-splosh!
Ker-sploosh!
The waves made going slow.

When Jesus finished with His prayers,
He wandered down the slope.
Wild winds were whipping back the boat.
His friends were losing hope.

Now, it was growing late, and it
was far around the lake.
But Jesus knew a better, faster path
that He could take.

He took a step.
He took one more.
Waves washed beneath His toes.

Ker-splish!
Ker-splash!
Ker-splosh!
Ker-sploosh!
on swells that dipped and rose.

The helpers huddled in the boat
that windy, stormy night.
They spied a ghost upon the lake.
It filled them all with fright.

Then Jesus called, "It's I!
Don't be afraid! Don't cry or shake!"
And Peter said, "Oh, Lord, I want
to walk upon the lake!"

"Then come!" called Jesus in reply.
So Peter took a leap.
Ker-splish!
Ker-splash!
Ker-splosh!
Ker-sploosh!
He walked on waters deep.

But then he saw the wind and waves,
and Peter started thinking.
He thought, *Oh, this will not be good!*
And then he started sinking!

So Jesus reached for Peter's hand
and asked him, "Why'd you doubt?
Oh, Peter, you of little faith."
And then He pulled him out.

The helpers sat inside the boat.
Their mouths were opened wide.
Ker-splish!
Ker-splash!
Ker-splosh!
Ker-sploosh!
The two then climbed inside.

At once the lake was smooth and calm!
The windy storm was done.
And all the helpers cheered,
"Oh truly, *You* are God's own Son!"

The Good Neighbor
The Parable of the Good Samaritan

Based on Luke 10:25-37

One day, Jesus was preaching and teaching God's Word.
A man stood to his feet so that he could be heard.
He said, "Teacher, I know that the law is quite clear.
If you want to see heaven, the rules are right here.

"They are: *Love the Lord God using all of your heart
and your soul and your strength and your mind—every part.
And you must love your neighbor the way you love you.*
Can you answer this question? My neighbor is who?"

Then Jesus said, "There was a guy who went walking.
He traveled a road where bad bandits were stalking.
The bandits attacked in a way that was rough.
They took all his clothes.
And they took all his stuff.

"They beat and they battered and walloped the guy.
Now, unable to move and too wounded to try,
lying flat on his back, he just stared at the sky.

"He just lay in the road, when along came a priest.
But the priest didn't give any help in the least.
No, the priest didn't care,
didn't stop,
didn't pray.
He just passed by the man and he went on his way.

"He just lay in the road simply wanting to cry,
when a man from the temple went scurrying by.
No, this man didn't care,
didn't stop,
didn't pray.
He just passed by the man and he went on his way.

"As he lay in the road, a Samaritan passed.
A chance to get help; maybe this was his last.
The Samaritan stopped and he did what he could.
He treated his wounds.
He was kind.
He was good.

"Then he carried the man to an inn for some rest.
He made sure that the care that he got was the best.
And he paid for it all,
every dollar and cent.
He paid for his food and his care and his rent.

"Now, the wounded man's neighbor
was one of the three
of the men on the road.
Tell me which could he be?"

"The man who gave help," was the fellow's reply.
Then Jesus said, "Go and behave like *that* guy."

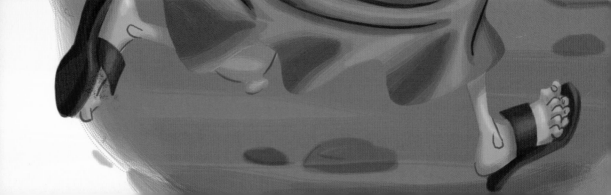

Lost and Found
The Parable of the Wayward Son

Based on Luke 15:11-32

One day, Jesus was preaching to sinners and such
when some teachers of law saw the crowd.
"He welcomes the sinners and eats with them too,"
they muttered with voices too loud.

Jesus told them this story:
"A man had two sons.
The youngest son said to his dad,
'Father, give to me now all the shares that are mine.'
He divided the wealth that he had.

"Soon the youngest son left with his money in hand.
He moved to a land far away.
He spent all his money on fanciful clothes,
and on food, and on drink, and on play.

"It didn't take long for his wealth to be gone,
then a famine came over the land.
The son had no money and nothing to eat,
and no one to lend him a hand.

"He needed a job, but the best he could find
was a job feeding piggies their slop.
With no food in his tummy, the slop sounded yummy.
He wanted the hunger to stop.

"He thought of the workers who worked for his dad—
They always have plenty to eat.
Instead of me starving, I'll go to my dad,
and I'll humble myself at his feet.

"I will say, 'I'm not worthy of being your son,
let me work as a servant instead.'
So he came to his senses and headed for home.
From the slop and the piggies he fled.

"His dad saw him coming while quite a way off.
He hurried to him at a run.
He hugged him and kissed him.
The boy said to his dad,
'I'm not worthy of being your son.'

"The dad told his servants, 'Now, quick! Bring a robe,
and bundle the robe 'round my son.
Put a ring on his finger
and shoes on his feet,
then cook up a feast when you're done.

"'My son who was lost is now found and at home.'
And everyone there started cheering.
When the older son finished his work and returned,
he said, 'What's all this music I'm hearing?'

"A servant explained that his brother had come
and his father had ordered a feast.
Now the brother got angry, refusing to go,
thinking this wasn't fair in the least.

"When his father came pleading for him to come in,
he said, 'Look! All these years I have slaved.
I've done all the stuff that you've asked me to do,
I've always been good and behaved.

"'I've not even gotten a goat for my work,
but my brother is given a feast.
Though he has been sinning and wasting your wealth
and not honoring you in the least.'

"'My son,' said the father, 'what's mine is all yours—
you've been home; you've stayed safe and stayed sound.
We must celebrate knowing your brother's alive.
Because he who was lost is now found!'"

Friends
The Lasting Story of the Last Supper

Based on Matthew 26:17-29, Mark 14:12-25,
Luke 22:7-20, John 13:21-35

Jesus sat with His friends and ate supper and talked.
Then He broke up some pieces of bread.
He gave thanks for the bread, then He passed it around.
"Take this. It's My body," He said.

Then He picked up His cup, and He blessed it and said,
"Drink this. It's My blood that's poured out.
It's for giving forgiveness of sins for the many."
They wondered what this was about.

Then glancing around at their faces He said,
"I will soon be betrayed by another."
His helpers asked, "Who is it? Surely not I?"
as they all looked around at each other.

"The one," Jesus said, "who dips bread in the bowl
at the *same* time as I. He's the guy."
Jesus dipped in the bowl.
Judas dipped in it too.
As he did, he said, "Surely not I?"

"Yes, it's you.
Quickly, do what it is you must do,"
said Jesus as Judas walked out.
The others sat watching and eating and talking.
They wondered what this was about.

He said, "Children, I'll only be here a short time.
I say to you, love one another.
Where *I* go, you *can't* go.
It's important you know
you must always show love to each other."

The Payment for Our Sins
The Incredible Story of Jesus on the Cross

Based on Matthew 26:3—27:54, Mark 14:32—15:39,
Luke 22:39—23:49, John 18:1—19:30

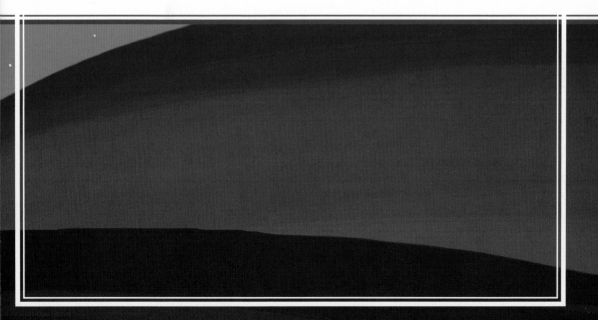

Some angry priests and leaders met
with wicked plans to make.
They wanted Jesus dead and gone,
believing Him a fake.

Then Jesus took His friends to find
a quiet place to pray.
The Mount of Olives seemed the perfect
place to get away.

There, Jesus said,
"Please watch and pray,"
then wandered off alone.
He found a place among the trees.
He knelt there on His own.

He said, "Oh, Father, if You could,
please take this cup away.
But it should be as You would wish
and not as I would say."

When He returned to find His friends,
He found that they were dozing.
They'd tried their best to watch and pray,
but soon their eyes were closing.

He said, "You couldn't watch an hour?"
But as His words came out,
a mob with torches, clubs, and swords
appeared all round about.

Then from the shadows, Judas stepped.
His kiss would be the cue,
the signal to the mob to start
the job they'd come to do.

The mob advanced with clubs and swords.
When they were getting near,
then Peter drew his sword and swung
and cut off someone's ear!

Then Jesus said, "Enough of this!"
and healed the injured ear.
He said, "All this is meant to be,
for *this* is why I'm here."

When Jesus stood before the priests,
they asked Him, "Tell us, do.
Are you the Christ, the Son of God?"
He answered, "Yes, it's true."

They thought that He had lied to them,
believing Him a fake.
They took Him to the governor.
Revenge they meant to take.

The governor, named Pilate, said,
"Jesus, tell me, do.
Are you the king of all the Jews?"
He answered, "Yes, it's true."

He hadn't broken any laws,
and Pilate told them so.
But still the leaders and the priests
said, "Jesus has to go!"

The leaders stirred the people up
into an angry mob.
They filled the people's hearts with hate
to finish off the job.

The people shouted, "Crucify!"
They wanted Jesus dead.
Though Pilate meant to set Him free,
he gave Him up instead.

Then soldiers mocked and beat Him up.
"Hail, king of Jews!" they said.
They made a pointy crown of thorns
and put it on His head.

They made Him drag a heavy cross—
although He barely could.
Then, laid Him out upon the cross
and nailed Him to the wood.

They raised His cross.
And there He died.
The sky turned black as night.
The ground began to shake and quake.
The guards cried out in fright.

The day He died was not the end.
Believe, and life begins!
For Jesus died for everyone,
the payment for our sins!

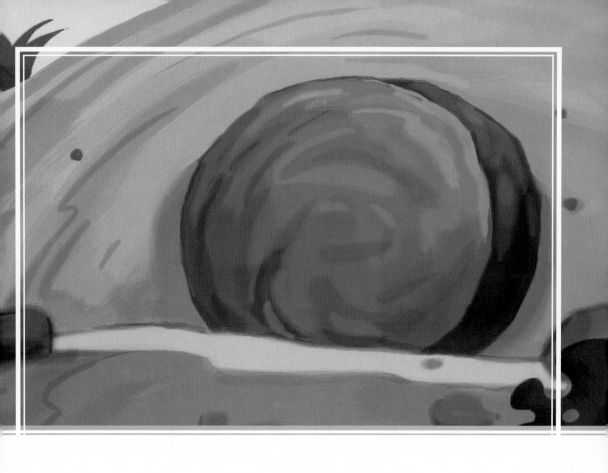

He Has Risen!

The Magnificent Story of the Resurrection

Based on Matthew 27:60—28:20, Mark 15:46—16:20, Luke 23:53—24:53, John 19:41—20:21, Acts 1:1-9

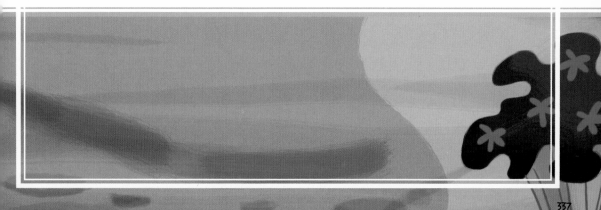

After Jesus had died, He was placed in a tomb.
It was sealed with a stone to keep thieves from the room.
Roman soldiers stood guard at the tomb, night and day,
so that no one could carry His body away.

Then on day number three, in the morning's first light,
the guards at the tomb had a terrible fright.
The earth began shaking and quaking and such,
their knees began knocking, they wobbled so much.

They were shocked.
They were spooked.
They were scared and alone.
But the worst thing of all ...
over there, by the stone ...
an angel appeared!
He was dressed all in white!
His clothes were as bright as a lightning bolt's light.

He pushed on the stone, and he rolled it aside.
They were too scared to speak.
They were too scared to hide.
They were too scared to run.
They decided instead ...

to just lie on the ground and pretend they were dead.

So they did. Then the angel just sat on the stone.
He just sat, and he waited, and left them alone.
Then three women arrived at the site of the tomb.
They were Jesus's friends. They brought spice and perfume.

But the stone had been moved.
And now, Jesus was gone.
They could see in the tomb by the light of the dawn.
Then the angel appeared.
He said, "Don't be afraid.
You are looking for Jesus.
He's not where He laid.

"He has risen! So go, and explain to His friends
and to Peter, the tomb's not the place where He ends."

When the women were where the eleven friends hid,
they described what they'd seen.
They described what they did.

But the friends thought it nonsense.
They didn't believe.
No way Jesus had simply decided to leave!
Well, they thought they should see
with their very own eyes.

So they did. And was *that* ever quite a surprise!
They saw for themselves that He wasn't inside.
Still, they couldn't believe that He lived,
though they tried.

Later, they hid from the Jews as before.
They closed all the shutters.
They bolted the door.

Then suddenly, Jesus was there in the room,
looking better than when He was laid in the tomb.
Now, was Jesus alive, or was Jesus a ghost?
It seemed to be Him.
Well, they thought so, almost.

Then He spoke to His friends.
He said, "Peace be with you."
And He tried to convince all His friends it was true.

He said, "Why are you troubled
and why do you doubt?
Just look at My hands and My feet.
Check them out.

"It is I, not a ghost.
Is a ghost bones and skin?
See the wound in My side?
Take your hand, put it in."

So they did. And at last all His friends really knew
what the women had said they had seen had been true!

So Jesus hung out with His friends for a while,
till the day that He left with a wave and a smile.
He said, "I must return to My Father above.
You must preach to the world about God's endless love.
You must preach the good news.
You must tell all creation,
and preach of salvation from sin to each nation."

Then He held out His hands and He lifted them high
and He blessed all His friends as He rose in the sky.

His friends all rejoiced as He floated to heaven.
Though Jesus had gone, He had left the eleven.
He'd told them to go and not hide as they'd hid,
and to preach the good news to the world.

So they did.